Once
upon a Rhyme

STORY RHYMES

Please visit our web site at: www.garethstevens.com
For a free color catalog describing Gareth Stevens Publishing's
list of high-quality books and multimedia programs, call
1-800-542-2595 (USA) or 1-800-387-3178 (Canada).
Gareth Stevens Publishing's fax: (414) 332-3567.

Library of Congress Cataloging-in-Publication Data available upon request from publisher.
Fax (414) 336-0157 for the attention of the Publishing Records Department.

ISBN 0-8368-4096-8

First published in 2004 by
Gareth Stevens Publishing
A World Almanac Education Group Company
330 West Olive Street, Suite 100
Milwaukee, Wisconsin 53212 USA

_612 729_

Copyright © 2004 by Nancy Hall, Inc.

Gareth Stevens series editor: Dorothy L. Gibbs
Gareth Stevens graphic designer: Kami M. Koenig

Printed in the United States of America

1 2 3 4 5 6 7 8 9 08 07 06 05 04

Once
upon a Rhyme

STORY RHYMES

by Matt Mitter • illustrations by Susan Banta

Gareth Stevens Publishing
A WORLD ALMANAC EDUCATION GROUP COMPANY

Rhyming words are fun!

Whenever you see two words like this:

PLANE ◆ CLOUD

choose the word that completes the rhyme.

Note: All word choices on each page are illustrated on that page.
When using this book with non-readers, point to the illustrations
and ask the children to say which one completes the rhyme.

Does your brother leave oodles of hair everywhere?
Do his six-inch-long claws cause the towels to tear?
Can he never sit down without breaking a chair?
Do his snarls and his growls give the neighbors a scare?
Does he chew up your shoes and your new underwear?

Does he leave, shall we say,
   a "strong smell" in the air?
If he does, then you probably ought to beware —
He's not really your brother at all. He's a
DOG ♦ BEAR!
(Say the correct word to finish the rhyme.)

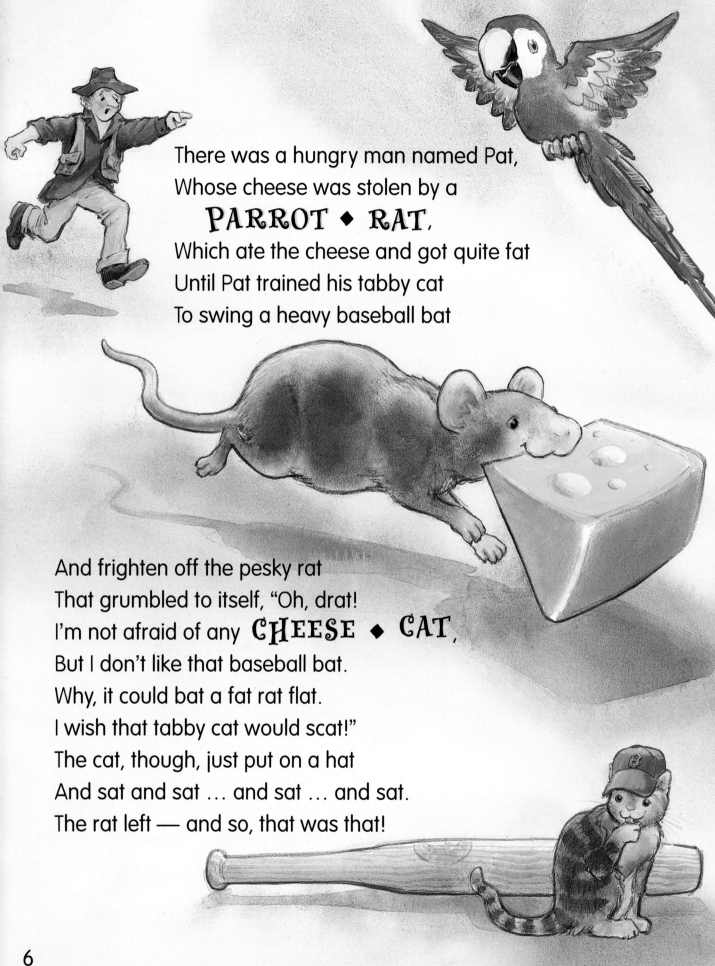

There was a hungry man named Pat,
Whose cheese was stolen by a
PARROT ◆ RAT,
Which ate the cheese and got quite fat
Until Pat trained his tabby cat
To swing a heavy baseball bat

And frighten off the pesky rat
That grumbled to itself, "Oh, drat!
I'm not afraid of any CHEESE ◆ CAT,
But I don't like that baseball bat.
Why, it could bat a fat rat flat.
I wish that tabby cat would scat!"
The cat, though, just put on a hat
And sat and sat … and sat … and sat.
The rat left — and so, that was that!

Jog! Jog! Heavy **TURTLE** ◆ **HOG**,
Through the misty morning fog,
Down the hill and 'cross the bog,

Past a howling shaggy
DOG ◆ **BIRD**,
Then, atop a hollow log.
Jog and jog and jog and jog!

7

Did you know Great-
aunt Lorraine
Lived in China, France,
and Spain?

She roller-skated in the rain.
She parachuted from a
PLANE ◆ CLOUD.
She hula-ed in a hurricane.

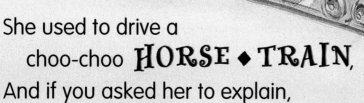

She used to drive a
choo-choo HORSE ◆ TRAIN,
And if you asked her to explain,
She'd say, "My dear, I'm not quite sane!"

8

High up in the shady trees,
There hummed a hive of bumble

SQUIRRELS ◆ BEES.
They suffered so from allergies
That all they did was wheeze and
SNEEZE ◆ SLEEP.
A doctor with advanced degrees
Advised them to eat cottage cheese
And lots and lots of fresh green peas.
In time, this cured the bees' disease.

There once was a doll that could sing.
It was made for a wealthy old **KING ◆ SAW**.

When the king wound its
SCREWDRIVER ◆ SPRING,
The doll sang everything,
But so loudly it made his ears ring!

Mary made a big mistake.
She went and bought herself a
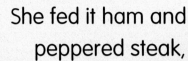 SNAKE ♦ LAMB.

She fed it ham and
peppered steak,

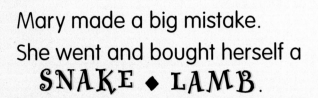

An extra-large vanilla shake,

And, then,
a slice of chocolate BREAD ♦ CAKE,
Which was another big mistake —
The poor snake got a stomachache!

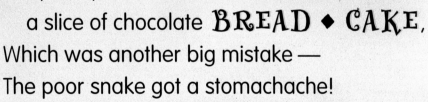

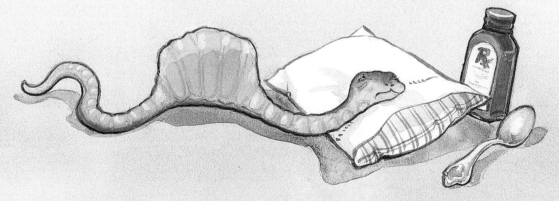

11

Fly high,
Little **BLIMP ◆ FLY**!
Try and try
To touch the sky.

Don't **LAUGH ◆ CRY**,
Little fly,
You'll be sky-high
By and by.

Dry your eye,
Little fly.

Fly and fly and fly —
Bye-bye!

There was an old woman who lived in a zoo,
Next door to a noisy and rude
OLD WOMAN ◆ KANGAROO.

So she packed up her children — she had twenty-two —

And moved them all into
a quiet old SHOE ◆ TENT.

Stop that stomping on the floor.
Quiet! Do not slam the
    DOOR ◆ **BALL**.
Don't whistle that way. Shh! No more!
You might wake up my
    TRAIN ◆ **DINOSAUR**,
And I would rather hear him snore
Than listen to his angry roar.

Oh, you can try, but what's the use?
You cannot tame a big, old
      MOUSE ◆ MOOSE.
He smacks, he spits, he spills his juice.

He breaks your favorite red caboose.
He comes home late with no excuse.
You're better off to turn him loose
And shout "Vamoose,

You silly DUCK ◆ GOOSE!"
You cannot tame that naughty moose.

15

To Parents and Teachers:

Having fun with language is easy and enjoyable, and when children play with rhyming words, they are actually gaining important reading skills. Try making up funny rhymes with children — the sillier the better! Pick almost any word and ask children to come up with as many rhyming words as they can. The picture quiz below is a good starting point for playing with rhyme.

Which word rhymes with hat?

MOOSE

CAT